POMPEII GUIDE 2024-2025

A Journey Through Time, Uncovering Ancient Treasures, Local Insights, and Hidden Stories of this Historic Roman City

Teresa Gilliam

Copyright © 2024 Teresa Gilliam All rights reserved.

No part of this book may be reproduced, stored in a retrieval system, or transmitted in any form or by any means, whether electronic, mechanical, photocopying, recording, scanning, or otherwise, without the publisher's prior written consent.

The work included herein is the sole property of the author and may not be reproduced or copied in any manner without the author's written consent. All information is provided "as is," without warranty of any kind, and liability is expressly disclaimed. The publisher and author expressly disclaim any duty for any loss, risk, or harm purportedly resulting from the use, application, or interpretation of the content contained herein.

MAP OF POMPEII

USE THE CODE TO SCAN FOR THE MAP

4 POMPEII TRAVEL GUIDE 2024-2025

TABLE OF CONTENTS

MAP OF POMPEII 3

INTRODUCTION TO POMPEII 9

    A BRIEF HISTORY 10

CHAPTER 1 12

    PLANNING YOUR TRIP 12

    BEST TIME TO VISIT 12

    HOW TO GET THERE 13

CHAPTER 2 16

    EXPLORING THE RUINS 16

    OVERVIEW OF THE ARCHAEOLOGICAL SITE 16

    1. MUST-SEE HIGHLIGHTS 16

    THE FORUM 16

    THE AMPHITHEATER 18

    THE VILLA OF THE MYSTERIES 19

    THE HOUSE OF THE FAUN 21

    THE GARDEN OF THE FUGITIVES 23

    GUIDED TOURS AND AUDIO GUIDES 24

    2. TIPS FOR VISITING 25

CHAPTER 3 29

EXPLORING MODERN POMPEII 29

LOCAL ATTRACTIONS AND MUSEUMS 29

POMPEII ARCHAEOLOGICAL PARK 33

ANTIQUARIUM OF POMPEII 36

THE SHRINE OF THE VIRGIN OF THE ROSARY 38

CHAPTER 4 40

EXPERIENCING POMPEII 40

WALKING TOURS 40

CYCLING ROUTES 43

CULTURAL EXPERIENCES 46

CHAPTER 5 49

ACCOMMODATION IN POMPEII 49

HOTELS 49

BED & BREAKFASTS 51

VACATION RENTALS 54

TIPS FOR BOOKING 57

CHAPTER 6 60

DINING IN POMPEII 60

LOCAL CUISINE 60

TOP RESTAURANTS 61

    CAFES AND STREET FOOD 66

CHAPTER 7 69

    SHOPPING IN POMPEII 69

    SOUVENIRS AND LOCAL CRAFTS 69

    MARKETS AND SHOPS 71

CHAPTER 8 75

    DAY TRIPS FROM POMPEII 75

    MOUNT VESUVIUS 75

    HERCULANEUM 77

    NAPLES 79

    SORRENTO AND THE AMALFI COAST 81

CHAPTER 9 84

    PRACTICAL INFORMATION 84

    HEALTH AND SAFETY TIPS 84

    ACCESSIBILITY INFORMATION 86

    EMERGENCY CONTACTS 87

CHAPTER 10 89

    USEFUL TIPS FOR TRAVELERS 89

    LANGUAGE AND COMMUNICATION 89

    CURRENCY AND PAYMENTS 91

LOCAL CUSTOMS AND ETIQUETTE 92

CHAPTER 11 95

POMPEII FOR FAMILIES 95

FAMILY-FRIENDLY ATTRACTIONS 95

ACTIVITIES FOR KIDS 98

CHAPTER 12 101

SUSTAINABLE TRAVEL IN POMPEII 101

ECO-FRIENDLY TIPS 101

RESPONSIBLE TOURISM PRACTICES 103

CONCLUSION 106

INTRODUCTION TO POMPEII

As the sun sets behind the haunting silhouette of Mount Vesuvius, its amber glow casts a spell over the ancient streets of Pompeii. I am an author and a seasoned traveler, drawn repeatedly to the profound mystery and poignant echoes of this once-bustling city, now frozen in time. Each visit unveils new secrets, whispers of the past that beckon the curious to explore deeper, to listen closer. This is not merely a guide; it is an invitation to journey through layers of history, to walk in the footsteps of Romans whose stories are immortalized in ash and stone.

Pompeii's tragic beauty and complex history have captivated my imagination, urging me to share its tales with fellow explorers. This book is crafted from years of exploration and learning, combined with insights gleaned from local experts and archaeologists who have dedicated their lives to understanding Pompeii's many layers. Whether you're wandering through the Forum, standing in the shadows of the amphitheater, or tracing the intricate mosaics in the Villa of the Mysteries, this guide will enhance your experience, providing context and detail that bring the ancient city alive.

Here, you'll find not just the paths to take, but the stories that make every ruin, every artifact, resonate with life. It's designed to help you navigate Pompeii's sprawling site with ease, ensuring that you don't miss any hidden gems or historical insights. From practical tips on travel and dining to thematic tours and hidden corners, this guide is your companion to experiencing Pompeii in its full, mesmerizing glory. Let's uncover the layers of history together, and make the most of every moment in this unforgettable place.

A BRIEF HISTORY

Pompeii, an ancient city in southern Italy, holds a significant place in history due to its tragic fate and its remarkably preserved ruins. Founded in the 7th or 6th century BCE by the Oscan people, Pompeii quickly became a thriving Roman city. Located near the Bay of Naples, it was a bustling center of commerce, culture, and daily life, reflecting the splendor of Roman civilization.

In 79 CE, the eruption of Mount Vesuvius brought an abrupt end to Pompeii's prosperity. The catastrophic event buried the city under a thick layer of volcanic ash and pumice, preserving it for centuries. This disaster, while devastating, has provided modern archaeologists with an unparalleled snapshot of ancient Roman life. The sudden burial of the city froze its buildings, artifacts, and even the unfortunate inhabitants in time, offering a detailed glimpse into daily life in a Roman city.

The rediscovery of Pompeii in 1748 sparked great interest and curiosity. Excavations revealed well-preserved homes, streets, public buildings, and artwork, showcasing the urban planning, architectural styles, and cultural practices of the time. The city's layout, with its forum, amphitheater, temples, and bathhouses, reveals the sophistication of Roman urban design and the importance of communal spaces in social life.

Walking through the ruins of Pompeii today, visitors can explore homes adorned with intricate mosaics and frescoes, visit the grand amphitheater where gladiators once fought, and see the remnants of bustling marketplaces and public baths. The plaster casts of the victims, created by filling the voids left in the ash, are a poignant reminder of the human cost of the disaster.

Pompeii's story is not just one of tragedy but also resilience and rediscovery. The preservation of the city offers invaluable insights into the daily lives, customs, and innovations of ancient Rome. It stands as a testament to human ingenuity and the enduring legacy of a civilization that continues to captivate and inspire people around the world.

CHAPTER 1

PLANNING YOUR TRIP

BEST TIME TO VISIT

Spring (March to May): Spring is one of the best times to visit Pompeii. The weather is mild and pleasant, perfect for exploring the ruins without the intense summer heat. The temperatures range from the mid-50s to the mid-70s Fahrenheit, making it comfortable to walk around and take in the sights. Additionally, the surrounding landscape comes to life with blooming flowers, adding a touch of natural beauty to the historic site.

Summer (June to August): Summer is the peak tourist season in Pompeii. The weather is hot, with temperatures often reaching the 90s. While the long days provide ample time to explore, the heat can be intense. If you choose to visit during the summer, plan to arrive early in the morning or late in the afternoon to avoid the midday sun. Despite the heat, summer offers the advantage of various cultural events and festivals in the nearby towns, enhancing your visit.

Fall (September to November): Fall is another excellent time to visit Pompeii. The temperatures are cooler than summer, ranging from the mid-60s to the low 80s, making it comfortable for sightseeing. The crowds thin out compared to the summer months, allowing for a more relaxed experience. Fall also brings a vibrant display of autumn colors in the surrounding areas, providing a picturesque backdrop to your visit.

Winter (December to February): Winter is the quietest time to visit Pompeii. The weather is cooler, with temperatures ranging from the low 40s to the mid-50s. While it can be chilly, the absence of large crowds offers a more intimate and peaceful exploration of the ruins. This season is ideal for those who prefer a quieter visit and want to take their time to absorb the history and atmosphere of the site.

HOW TO GET THERE

Getting to Pompeii by Train

The train is the most popular and convenient way to reach Pompeii. If you are beginning from Naples, proceed to the Napoli Centrale station. From there, take the Circumvesuviana train on the Napoli-Sorrento line and get off at the Pompei Scavi - Villa dei Misteri station. The travel takes about 35 minutes, and trains run regularly, making it easy to arrange your visit.

Arriving by Bus

For those who like buses, there are various options available. From Naples, you can use the EAV bus service, which departs from Piazza Garibaldi, near the Napoli Centrale rail station. The bus travel takes roughly 45 minutes and drops you right near the entrance to the ancient site.

Traveling by Car

Driving to Pompeii offers flexibility and the opportunity to explore the surrounding surroundings. From Naples, take the A3 motorway towards Salerno and exit at Pompei Ovest. Follow the markers to the archaeological site. There are various parking lots available near the entrances, though they can fill up rapidly, especially during high tourist season.

Guided Tours and Private Transfers

For a more personalized experience, consider taking a guided tour or private shuttle. Many tour providers in Naples offer packages that include transportation and a guided tour of Pompeii. This option is convenient and often delivers informative comments from qualified guides, improving your stay.

Tips for a Smooth Journey

1. Plan Ahead: Check the train and bus schedules in advance to ensure flawless travel.

2. Start Early: Arriving early helps you escape the noon throng and the heat, making your visit more comfortable.

3. Bring Essentials: Carry water, sunscreen, and a hat, as there is limited shade within the ancient site.

4. Comfy Footwear: Wear strong, comfy shoes, as you will be strolling on uneven ancient streets.

CHAPTER 2

EXPLORING THE RUINS

OVERVIEW OF THE ARCHAEOLOGICAL SITE

1. MUST-SEE HIGHLIGHTS

THE FORUM

The Forum of Pompeii is an essential visit for anybody interested in ancient Roman history. Located in the heart of the ancient city, the Forum was the hub of political, economic, and social life. Walking through this huge site gives you a feeling of how life once bustled in this now-silent ruin.

The Forum is flanked by spectacular monuments, including temples, government offices, and marketplaces. One of the most remarkable buildings is the Temple of Jupiter, which stands conspicuously at the northern end. This temple was devoted to the monarch of the Roman gods and functioned as a symbol of Roman sovereignty and religion. Nearby, the Basilica was a place where justice was administered and commerce transactions were performed, showing the dual role of public structures in ancient times.

As you explore, you'll find the relics of the Macellum, the primary market of Pompeii. Here, locals would have come every day to buy fresh produce, meats, and seafood. The ruins of the market booths and storage rooms provide an insight into the daily lives of Pompeii's people.

The Forum was not merely a center of commerce and governance; it was also a social magnet. The central open space would have been filled with citizens engaging in debates, public speeches, and social events. The columns and statues that originally graced this region hint at its former grandeur and the importance of public life in Roman society.

Preserved under layers of ash from the cataclysmic eruption of Mount Vesuvius in AD 79, the Forum offers a unique look at Roman urban planning and construction. The precise arrangement and the complex infrastructure, such as the intricate water systems and the public baths, highlight the sophistication of Roman engineering.

Visiting the Forum now, you can still see the paving stones of the streets and the outlines of structures that have been excavated. Informative signs and guided tours provide context, letting you comprehend the significance of each structure and the daily activities that take place here.

THE AMPHITHEATER

The Amphitheater at Pompeii is a marvel of ancient Roman engineering and a crucial feature for any tourist viewing the archeological site. Built-in 70 BC, it is one of the oldest surviving Roman amphitheaters in the world and offers a look into the vibrant social and cultural life of ancient Pompeii.

As you step into the amphitheater, you'll be taken back to a time when gladiatorial contests and public spectacles captivated the residents of Pompeii. The edifice could hold up to 20,000 people, showcasing the prominence of these events in Roman culture. The elliptical design and tiered seating gave great views from every aspect, making it an architectural accomplishment of its day.

Walking into the amphitheater, you can practically hear the echoes of the thundering spectators and the clash of gladiators' swords. The arena floor, formerly covered with sand to sponge up the blood from combat, today serves as a peaceful reminder of the terrible yet interesting past. This historic amphitheater not only housed gladiator contests but also other sorts of entertainment such as animal hunts and public executions.

The architecture of the amphitheater incorporates various revolutionary features for its time, such as the velarium, a wide awning that could be stretched over the sitting area to offer shade for spectators. This edifice displays the Romans' excellent understanding of design and their ability to create useful yet spectacular public areas.

Exploring the amphitheater, you can also discover the vestiges of the halls and hallways that gladiators and animals used to enter the arena. These behind-the-scenes locations give another degree of complexity to the site, allowing you to visualize the preparations and tension before each event.

The Amphitheater in Pompeii is not merely a relic of the past but a witness to the city's once-thriving community. It stands as a symbol of the entertainment and social activities that were fundamental to Roman society. Visiting this location offers a unique opportunity to interact with history and develop a deeper understanding of the people who formerly came here to witness amazing spectacles.

THE VILLA OF THE MYSTERIES

The Villa of the Mysteries is one of the most fascinating archaeological sites in Pompeii, affording a peek into the ancient world that is both intriguing and awe-inspiring. This well-preserved mansion is located just outside the city walls and is famed for its beautiful murals that portray mystery ceremonies related to the cult of Dionysus, the god of wine.

Dating back to the 2nd century BC, the Villa of the Mysteries was initially a stately mansion that subsequently grew into a sumptuous retreat. The edifice showcases the wealth and refinement of its owners, having multiple rooms and courtyards that were utilized for both living and partying. Visitors can stroll around these chambers and imagine the daily lives of the villa's inhabitants, getting a fuller understanding of Roman household architecture and lifestyle.

One of the most notable characteristics of the villa is its murals, which adorn the walls of the triclinium, or eating room. These paintings are colorful and well-preserved, affording a rare glimpse into the religious activities and creative traditions of the time. The frescoes portray a series of rituals, probably initiation ceremonies, relating to the Dionysian mysteries. The vibrant colors and detailed intricacies of the artwork attract tourists, making the home a must-see for anybody interested in ancient art and religion.

The site also offers a range of additional rooms, each with its distinct qualities. From the kitchen, with its ancient cooking implements, to the peristyle, a courtyard ringed by columns, every component of the home reveals a tale of life in ancient Pompeii. The painstaking excavation and preservation efforts allow visitors to travel back in time and see this magnificent mansion as it once was.

To make the most of your visit to the Villa of the Mysteries, it is advisable to join a guided tour. Knowledgeable guides can provide in-depth explanations of the frescoes and the historical context of the villa, enriching the whole experience. Additionally, the villa's location affords spectacular views of the surrounding area, contributing to the sense of connection with the past.

THE HOUSE OF THE FAUN

The House of the Faun is one of the most impressive and large mansions in Pompeii, affording tourists a peek into the luxury lifestyle of the city's elite before the devastating explosion of Mount Vesuvius in 79 AD. This enormous villa, spanning a whole city block, is a tribute to the riches and sophistication of its owners.

Built in the 2nd century BC, the House of the Faun is famed for its magnificent architecture and stunning mosaics. The name of the house is taken from a bronze statue of a dancing faun located in the impluvium, the central pool of the atrium. This figure is a feature of the home, embodying the artistic and cultural triumphs of Pompeii.

The House of the Faun is separated into two main portions, each with its collection of rooms and gardens. The first section is the older part of the home, while the second half was constructed later, representing the expansion and rising affluence of the family. Visitors can meander through several gorgeously adorned rooms, each showing elaborate mosaics and frescoes that have impressively survived through the decades.

The Alexander Mosaic, which shows King Darius III of Persia and Alexander the Great engaged in the Battle of Issus, is one of the most well-known mosaics in the House of the Faun. This masterpiece, constructed of millions of tiny tesserae, is a beautiful example of ancient artistry and craftsmanship. Although the original is currently held at the National Archaeological Museum of Naples, a reproduction can be seen in the house itself, allowing visitors to understand its historical value.

The House of the Faun also has two huge peristyle gardens, encircled by columns and ornamented with different statues and fountains. These gardens provided a tranquil getaway for the locals, offering a spot for leisure and social meetings. The combination of open spaces and intricate decorations produces a feeling of elegance and peace.

Walking around the House of the Faun, tourists can imagine the daily lives of Pompeii's elite. The layout and style of the home reflect the Roman emphasis on hospitality and entertainment, with abundant room for hosting guests and conducting business. The splendor of the home is a tribute to the riches and cultural richness of ancient Pompeii.

THE GARDEN OF THE FUGITIVES

The Garden of the Fugitives, located in the southern portion of Pompeii, is a haunting yet interesting location. This region, once a lovely garden, became the ultimate resting place for 13 persons attempting to escape the terrible eruption. Their remains were covered in ash, producing cavities that were later filled with plaster by archaeologists. This technology has yielded realistic casts of the victims, documenting their dying moments with startling clarity.

Walking through the Garden of the Fugitives, tourists can observe these casts displayed in situ, surrounded by the relics of the garden that once thrived there. The scene is both poignant and enlightening, establishing a palpable connection to the past. It's a vivid reminder of the suddenness of the calamity and the humanity of its victims.

The garden itself has been partially restored, giving visitors a taste of its original magnificence. The precise planting of plants and flowers reflects those that would have been present in ancient times, presenting a tranquil contrast to the horror honored here. This restoration project aims to highlight daily life in Pompeii, showing how the citizens tended their gardens and appreciated nature.

The Garden of the Fugitives provides unique information into Roman horticulture and the varieties of plants that were cultivated in Pompeii. This component of the site highlights the importance of gardens in Roman culture, not merely as sources of food but as locations for relaxation and interaction.

The Garden of the Fugitives is a major component of any visit to Pompeii, offering a unique blend of natural beauty, historical relevance, and emotional depth. It allows visitors to engage with the ancient world in a deeply personal way, providing a glimpse into the lives and deaths of the people who lived there. This site is not simply a monument to those who lost but also a celebration of the tenacity and continuance of life.

GUIDED TOURS AND AUDIO GUIDES

Since the large site can be daunting, audio guides and guided tours are highly advised. Skilled tour leaders breathe life into history by narrating tales of the local inhabitants, the devastating eruption, and the excavation work done at the site. These excursions offer insights that aren't immediately apparent from simply observing the remains, like specifics of the building methods, the historical significance of particular structures, and the day-to-day activities of the Pompeiian populace.

An adaptable substitute that lets guests explore at their speed is an audio guide. These comprehensive tutorials, which are available in several languages, give you context and commentary as you navigate the website. They are simple to use, and the numbered areas of interest match the thorough descriptions, so you won't miss any important details.

There are specialty excursions that concentrate on particular facets of Pompeii, such as its art, architecture, or the life of its citizens, for visitors seeking a more in-depth experience. These tours provide a better understanding of the cultural and historical significance of the city by covering regions that are typically left out of normal tours.

2. TIPS FOR VISITING

Plan Ahead

Before heading to Pompeii, it's a good idea to arrange your visit. Purchase your tickets online to avoid huge lineups at the entry. Consider downloading a map of the site and marking the important sections you want to investigate. This will help you make the most of your time and guarantee you don't miss any crucial sites.

Wear Comfortable Clothing and Footwear

Pompeii is a big ancient site with uneven ground, therefore suitable shoes are a requirement. Opt for breathable clothing, as the temperature may be extremely warm, especially in the summer months. Remember to protect yourself from the sun by wearing a hat and sunscreen.

Stay Hydrated and Bring Snacks

There are limited locations to buy food and drinks inside the site, so it's recommended to carry your water bottle and some snacks. Staying hydrated is crucial, as the sun can be harsh and walking difficult.

Arrive Early or Late

To avoid the throng and the heat, try to visit Pompeii early in the morning or later in the day. These hours are not only cooler but also offer excellent lighting for pictures.

Get a Guide or Listen to a Guidebook

While you can visit Pompeii on your own, hiring a guide or employing an audio guide can considerably enhance your experience. These tours provide significant insights into the history and significance of the ruins, making your visit more interesting and entertaining.

Respect the Site

Pompeii is a precious historical resource. Be considerate by not touching the ruins or removing any relics. Stick to the specified routes and avoid climbing on the structures to protect the place for future generations.

Visit the Must-See Spots

Some sites of Pompeii are extremely interesting and should not be ignored. These include the Forum, the Amphitheater, the Villa of the Mysteries, and the House of the Faun. Each of these venues offers a unique view into distinct facets of Roman life.

Take Your Time

Pompeii is a place to relish. Take your time to explore, absorb the ambiance, and envision what life was like in this old metropolis. Don't rush from one site to another; instead, allow yourself to be taken back in time.

Be Prepared for Limited Accessibility

Keep in mind that due to its ancient structure, Pompeii has limited accessibility for people with mobility impairments. While some places are accessible, many parts involve walking on uneven surfaces and ascending steps.

Check the Weather

Before you go, check the weather forecast. Pompeii can be very hot in the summer and can occasionally encounter rain. If required, wear appropriate clothing and bring a raincoat or umbrella.

Combine Your Visit

Consider combining your visit to Pompeii with a tour of the adjacent Mount Vesuvius or the Naples National Archaeological Museum. Both offer new insights into the region's history and the tragic explosion that buried Pompeii.

Capture the Memories

Finally, bring a nice camera or smartphone to capture your experience. The ruins provide several photo opportunities that you'll want to remember. Just be aware of other guests when shooting pictures.

CHAPTER 3

EXPLORING MODERN POMPEII
LOCAL ATTRACTIONS AND MUSEUMS

1. The Ruins of Pompeii

Location: Via Villa dei Misteri, 2, 80045 Pompeii NA, Italy

Description: The Ruins of Pompeii are the heart of the city's historical allure. Buried under volcanic ash from Mount Vesuvius in 79 AD, this archaeological site provides a unique glimpse into ancient Roman life. You can wander through well-preserved streets, homes, and public buildings, including the Forum, the Amphitheater, and the Villa of the Mysteries.

Tips: Wear comfortable walking shoes as the site is expansive and involves a lot of walking on uneven surfaces. Arrive early to avoid the midday crowds and bring water, especially during the hot summer months.

Prices: Adult tickets are approximately €16, with discounts available for children, students, and seniors.

2. The Pompeii Archaeological Park

Location: Via Villa dei Misteri, 80045 Pompeii NA, Italy

Description: This expansive park includes the ruins and several key structures, such as the Temple of Apollo and the House of the Faun. Each building tells its own story through detailed frescoes, mosaics, and artifacts.

Tips: Consider hiring a guide or using an audio guide for a more comprehensive understanding of the history and significance of each site. Plan your visit around the weather, as many parts of the park are open-air.

Prices: Entry to the park is included in the general admission ticket to the ruins, priced at €16.

3. The Pompeii Forum

Location: Located within the Pompeii Ruins

Description: The Forum was the political, economic, and religious center of Pompeii. Surrounded by important buildings like the Basilica and the Temple of Jupiter, it offers insights into the civic life of ancient Pompeii.

Tips: Spend time exploring the different sections of the Forum to appreciate its scale and importance. For photography, early morning trips provide the greatest light.

Prices: Included in the general admission ticket to the ruins.

4. The Antiquarium of Pompeii

Location: Via Villa dei Misteri, 2, 80045 Pompeii NA, Italy

Description: The Antiquarium serves as a museum within the archaeological park, displaying artifacts recovered from the site. Exhibits include pottery, jewelry, and tools, offering a tangible connection to the lives of Pompeii's residents.

Tips: Allocate at least an hour to explore the museum. It's a good idea to visit the Antiquarium either at the start or end of your visit to provide context for what you see in the ruins.

Prices: Included in the general admission ticket to the ruins.

5. Villa of the Mysteries

Location: Via Villa dei Misteri, 2, 80045 Pompeii NA, Italy

Description: This well-preserved villa is famous for its stunning frescoes, which depict mysterious initiation rites. The vibrant colors and detailed scenes provide a rare look at Roman art and religious practices.

Tips: The villa is located a bit off the main path, so plan your route accordingly. Photography is allowed, but flash is prohibited to protect the frescoes.

Prices: Included in the general admission ticket to the ruins.

6. The Forum Baths

Location: Located within the Pompeii Ruins

Description: The Forum Baths are some of the best-preserved structures in Pompeii. These public baths were an integral part of daily life, and you can see the various rooms including the frigidarium (cold room), tepidarium (warm room), and caldarium (hot room).

Tips: Look for the intricate ceiling decorations and the heating system that highlights Roman engineering prowess. To beat the crowd, it's advisable to arrive early.

Prices: Included in the general admission ticket to the ruins.

7. Pompeii Amphitheater

Location: Located within the Pompeii Ruins

Description: One of the earliest Roman amphitheaters still standing is the Pompeii Amphitheater. It was utilized for public events such as gladiatorial contests and could accommodate up to 20,000 spectators.

Tips: Climb to the top tiers for a panoramic view of the structure and the surrounding ruins. Consider bringing a hat and sunscreen as there is little shade.

Prices: Included in the general admission ticket to the ruins.

8. House of the Faun

Location: Located within the Pompeii Ruins

Description: The House of the Faun is one of the largest and most impressive residences in Pompeii, named after the bronze statue of a dancing faun found in the atrium. The house is renowned for its exquisite mosaics, including the famous Alexander Mosaic.

Tips: Take your time to explore the various rooms and gardens. The mosaics are delicate, so avoid touching them.

Prices: Included in the general admission ticket to the ruins.

POMPEII ARCHAEOLOGICAL PARK

An amazing window into the past, the Pompeii Archaeological Park gives tourists a rare look into an ancient world preserved in time. Situated in the Italian city of Pompeii, close to Naples, this ancient monument is among the world's most well-known archeological sites.

Before being destroyed by volcanic ash and pumice in 79 AD due to Mount Vesuvius' tragic eruption, Pompeii was a thriving Roman metropolis. The Pompeii remains, which have been incredibly well preserved for nearly two millennia, offer an amazing chronicle of daily life in the Roman Empire.

A wide range of exquisitely preserved buildings, including residences, temples, and public spaces, are open for exploration by park visitors. One of the most striking sights is the Villa of the Mysteries, which is well-known for its intricate murals that show enigmatic rituals and celebrations. Because they provide insight into the cultural and religious traditions of the era, these artworks have enthralled both tourists and historians.

Another feature is the Forum, which served as the hub of public life in ancient Pompeii. The remnants of significant public structures, including the basilica, temples, and marketplaces, are visible to tourists here. You can practically hear the commotion of traders and people going about their everyday business as you go around the Forum.

One of the oldest Roman amphitheaters still standing is the Amphitheater, which is a must-see. It used to be the site of gladiatorial matches and other events that gave Pompeii residents enjoyment. It is simple to picture the crowd's clamor as they supported their favorite gladiators while standing in this historic arena.

Pompeii's sophisticated infrastructure, which includes an intricate network of aqueducts and baths, is yet another amazing aspect. Among the best preserved are the Stabian Baths, which provide an insight into the opulent way of life that the city's wealthy citizens enjoyed. The elaborate murals and mosaic flooring serve as reminders of the era's skill and expertise.

The House of the Faun is a must-visit location for anybody curious about Pompeii's everyday life. Beautiful mosaics, featuring the well-known picture of Alexander the Great fighting, adorn this opulent home. The interior design and furnishings of the house paint a vivid image of Roman household life, reflecting the wealth and rank of its owners.

The plaster casts of the eruption victims are among the most emotional features of a trip to Pompeii. Plaster was poured into the spaces created in the ash by the decaying bodies to create these casts. The resulting figures, which depict their last moments in a striking and poignant display, serve as eerie reminders of the catastrophe that befell the citizens of the city.

More than just a scattering of ruins, the Pompeii Archaeological Park is a vivid representation of human history and tenacity. Visitors are taken back in time as they stroll through the historic streets, where they may learn more about the struggles, successes, and daily lives of the locals.

ANTIQUARIUM OF POMPEII

The Antiquarium of Pompeii, a cornerstone of the ancient city's exploration, is an essential visit for those captivated by history. Situated at the gateway of the Pompeii Archaeological Park, this museum gives an enlightening trip through the daily life, culture, and sad end of Pompeii.

Exhibits and Artifacts

The museum's displays provide a detailed look at the city's history, from its early days until its disastrous destruction in 79 AD. Among the presented exhibits are common things, creative works, and personal belongings that reflect life in ancient Pompeii. The museum has an outstanding collection of frescoes, sculptures, and mosaics, each narrating a distinct story of the past.

Interactive Displays

Interactive displays and multimedia installations enrich the experience, allowing visitors to participate in the exhibitions in a modern and dynamic way. These elements bring the ancient city to life, making it simpler to appreciate the context and value of the items.

Educational Value

The Antiquarium is not simply about viewing items; it's an educational resource that offers deep insights into Roman culture and society. Informative panels and audio guides provide thorough explanations, increasing the visitor's comprehension of the items and their historical context.

Accessibility

The museum is designed to be accessible to all visitors, especially those with mobility difficulties. Its layout guarantees that everyone will appreciate the displays easily. Additionally, the staff is kind and informed, ready to assist with any queries or requirements.

Visiting Tips

Plan to spend at least a couple of hours touring the Antiquarium to truly appreciate its huge collection. Arriving early might help avoid the crowds and create a more comfortable experience. Consider employing an audio guide for a more in-depth knowledge of the exhibits.

THE SHRINE OF THE VIRGIN OF THE ROSARY

Travelers seeking both spiritual development and historical understanding will find the Shrine of the Virgin of the Rosary in Pompeii to be a stunning and noteworthy location. Nestled in the center of Pompeii, this shrine draws millions of pilgrims and tourists each year with its striking architecture, fascinating history, and spiritual significance.

The shrine has an intriguing tale of faith and devotion, having been founded in the late 1800s by Bartolo Longo, a lawyer who became a lay Dominican. Building this shrine was Longo's lifelong endeavor, motivated by his profound empathy for the plight of the underprivileged and the spiritual needs of the local populace. Several gifts from all across the world helped him in his endeavors, enabling the building of this amazing church.

Viewed from a distance, the towering bell tower of the shrine marks its exterior and acts as a beacon for onlookers. The elaborate features of the front, which are embellished with statues and reliefs that portray events from the lives of Christ and the Virgin Mary, will become apparent as you go closer. The main entryway is imposing and welcoming, ushering you into the hallowed area inside.

The shrine is just as breathtaking inside. Vast and roomy, the nave boasts high ceilings and exquisite stained glass windows that let in an abundance of natural light and foster a calm and reflective ambiance within. The altar, the center of attention in the church, is beautifully crafted and embellished with priceless materials, expressing the reverence and devotion of the devout who gather here to worship.

Housed in a private chapel, the miraculous image of the Virgin of the Rosary is one of the most outstanding characteristics of the shrine. Many pilgrims flock to this image, which is said to have worked many miracles, to pray and ask for favors. Many times, people who have felt the Virgin's intercession leave candles and flowers in the chapel.

The shrine has a museum that provides more insight into its background and significance. Visitors can view a variety of religious artifacts here, such as chalices, vestments, and other liturgical objects. The museum offers a stimulating and educational experience that aids in visitors' appreciation of this hallowed location's cultural and spiritual legacy.

The shrine serves as a hub for humanitarian and social service endeavors in addition to its religious purposes. The church offers healthcare services, educational programs, and aid to the underprivileged as part of its efforts to support the neighborhood. This feature of the shrine emphasizes its goal to meet the needs of the people on a spiritual and material level.

CHAPTER 4

EXPERIENCING POMPEII

WALKING TOURS

Discovering Pompeii's Highlights

Start your trip at the main entrance, Porta Marina, which brings you into the heart of Pompeii. The Forum, once the hub of public life, is an excellent location to begin. Here, you can observe the remnants of temples, government buildings, and marketplaces. The expansive space affords a clear perspective of the social and political heart of ancient Pompeii.

Exploring the Streets and Homes

Walking along the cobbled streets, you'll discover the well-preserved structures that previously housed the city's population. The House of the Faun is particularly striking with its exquisite mosaics and vast layout. Nearby, the Villa of the Mysteries contains magnificently conserved murals depicting enigmatic initiation procedures. These homes provide insight into the daily lives and cultural traditions of Pompeii's inhabitants.

Visiting Public Baths and Theaters

Pompeii's public baths, such as the Stabian Baths, offer an insight into the leisure activities of the ancient Romans. These baths were not merely locations for bathing but also for socializing and conducting business. The Grand Theater and the smaller Odeon were places for plays and public meetings, showcasing the city's robust cultural life.

Discovering the Temples and Religious Sites

Religious practices were important to life in Pompeii. The Temple of Apollo and the Temple of Jupiter are prominent sites that reflect the city's devotion to its gods. These temples are marked by their towering columns and elaborate altars, reflecting the architectural brilliance of the time.

Exploring the Commercial Areas

The Macellum (market) and the stores along Via dell'Abbondanza illustrate Pompeii's commercial activity. Walking through these districts, you can almost hear the rush and bustle of businesses and consumers. The Lupanar, an old brothel, is another important landmark that offers a frank view into the more personal parts of Roman society.

Enjoying the Views from the Amphitheater

End your journey at the Amphitheater, one of the oldest surviving Roman amphitheaters. It could seat up to 20,000 spectators and was used for gladiatorial contests and other public performances. The view from the top offers a panoramic overview of the entire archaeological site.

Tips for a Memorable Visit

1. Wear Comfortable Shoes: The historic streets are uneven, and you'll be doing a lot of walking.

2. Bring Water and Snacks: There are limited amenities inside the site, so it's best to come prepared.

3. Use a Map: Pompeii is large, and a map will help you traverse its various attractions.

4. Hire a Guide or Use an Audio Guide: To obtain a greater understanding of the site's history and significance.

CYCLING ROUTES

Discovering Pompeii's Highlights

Start your trip at the main entrance, Porta Marina, which brings you into the heart of Pompeii. The Forum, once the hub of public life, is an excellent location to begin. Here, you can observe the remnants of temples, government buildings, and marketplaces. The expansive space affords a clear perspective of the social and political heart of ancient Pompeii.

Route 1: The Ancient City Loop

This route takes you into the center of Pompeii, allowing you to visit the most iconic sites while enjoying a leisurely ride. Start from the main entrance and pedal towards the Forum, the central plaza of ancient Pompeii. From there, go to the Amphitheater, one of the oldest surviving Roman amphitheaters. This loop is generally flat and ideal for all skill levels, making it perfect for families and casual riders.

Route 2: The Coastal Path

For those who want to appreciate the splendor of the shore, this path offers spectacular views of the Bay of Naples. Begin your ride at the Pompeii ruins and travel towards the coast, passing through luscious vineyards and olive groves. Once you reach the shoreline, continue the walkway that goes alongside the sea, affording stunning sights and a cool sea wind. This path is a little harder due to some modest hills but is well worth the effort.

Route 3: The Countryside Trail

If you prefer a more rural setting, the countryside walk is great. This path takes you through the lovely countryside surrounding Pompeii. Start your tour from the city center and head towards the countryside, where you'll ride through picturesque villages and fields of wildflowers. The trail is generally level with a few rolling hills, allowing a tranquil and scenic ride away from the throng.

Route 4: The Mount Vesuvius Challenge

For experienced cyclists searching for a more strenuous ride, the Mount Vesuvius Challenge is a necessity. Begin your journey in Pompeii and pedal towards the base of the famed volcano. The hike to the top is steep and demanding, but the panoramic views from the summit are truly rewarding. Be sure to bring lots of water and take breaks as required, as this route can be physically challenging.

Route 5: The Historical Journey

This trip mixes history and cycling, leading you to several lesser-known but equally intriguing places around Pompeii. Start at the main entrance and pedal towards the Villa of the Mysteries, a well-preserved Roman villa with beautiful frescoes. From there, continue to the House of the Faun, one of the largest and most beautiful homes in Pompeii. This route is relatively easy, with well-paved routes and modest climbs.

Tips for Cycling in Pompeii

1. Safety First: Always wear a helmet and respect local traffic rules. Pompeii's streets might be tiny and congested, so keep vigilant and ride cautiously.

2. Stay Hydrated: The Mediterranean climate can be scorching, especially in the summer. Carry enough water and take breaks to stay hydrated.

3. Respect the Sites: Pompeii is a UNESCO World Heritage site with fragile ruins. Stick to approved trails and avoid cycling too close to the ruins to help preserve them.

4. Bike Rentals: There are various bike rental businesses in Pompeii where you may discover a variety of bicycles to suit your needs, from mountain bikes to city cruisers.

5. Greatest Time to Ride: Early mornings and late afternoons are the greatest times to cycle, as the weather is cooler and the crowds are lighter.

CULTURAL EXPERIENCES

Exploring the Ancient Ruins

Wandering around the streets of Pompeii, you may view the well-preserved relics of ancient buildings, including dwellings, stores, and public baths. The architecture and arrangement provide insights into Roman urban planning and daily life. Key sites include the Forum, the core of political and social life, and the Amphitheater, one of the oldest of its kind, which held gladiatorial games and other shows.

Visiting the House of the Faun

One of Pompeii's greatest mansions, the House of the Faun, offers a peek into the lavish lifestyle of the elite. The building is famed for its exquisite mosaics, especially the famous "Alexander Mosaic," showing a war scene between Alexander the Great and Darius III. These elaborate artworks reflect the artistic achievements and cultural values of the time.

Admiring the Frescoes of the Villa of the Mysteries

The Villa of the Mysteries is known for its vibrant paintings, which are among the best-preserved artworks from ancient Rome. These paintings portray mystery ceremonies, presumably tied to the cult of Dionysus, offering an intriguing insight into religious practices and beliefs. The colors and intricacies of the paintings have weathered the test of time, delivering a spectacular visual experience.

Strolling at the Garden of the Fugitives

This heartbreaking area comprises plaster casts of victims of the eruption, caught in their dying moments. The Garden of the Fugitives not only acts as a dramatic reminder of the human cost of the calamity but also demonstrates the ingenious approaches utilized by archaeologists to preserve these terrible figures. It is a poignant event that gives depth to the historical understanding of Pompeii.

Exploring the Bathhouses

The public bathhouses of Pompeii, such as the Stabian Baths, illustrate the social and cultural importance of bathing in Roman culture. These facilities were not merely locations for bathing but also social hubs where people congregated to rest and socialize. The elaborate heating systems, mosaic floors, and frescoed walls highlight the brilliance of Roman engineering and craftsmanship.

Dining Like the Romans

While at Pompeii, don't miss the chance to try ancient Roman cuisine. Several local eateries offer dishes inspired by recipes from ancient times, allowing you to enjoy the pleasures that once thrilled Pompeii's population. This culinary experience ties you to the past in a concrete and tasty way.

Exploring the Pompeii Archaeological Park

The Pompeii Archaeological Park provides detailed insights into the city's history and culture. With its rich collection of antiquities, the park's museums and exhibitions help put together the story of Pompeii's growth and demise. Guided tours are available for individuals who seek to expand their awareness of the site's significance.

Attending Cultural Events and Performances

Pompeii features different cultural events and performances throughout the year, including theater productions and concerts staged in the old theater. These activities bring the ruins to life, allowing you to experience the place as the Romans might have, with music and drama filling the historic halls.

Learning at the Antiquarium

The Antiquarium of Pompeii is a museum that showcases artifacts found on the site, adding more context and history. Exhibits include common things, such as pottery and utensils, as well as more elaborate pieces, including jewelry and sculptures. This museum provides a deeper knowledge of the people who formerly lived in Pompeii.

CHAPTER 5

ACCOMMODATION IN POMPEII

HOTELS

1. Hotel Diana Pompei

Hotel Diana Pompei offers a blend of modern conveniences and ancient charm. The rooms are spacious and well-appointed, giving a quiet hideaway after a day of sightseeing. Located just a short walk from the ancient ruins, this hotel is ideally located for exploring. Prices range from $70 to $120 per night, making it an economical option for vacationers. For reservations, call +39 081 850 7155.

2. Resort Bosco De' Medici

Nestled in a secluded area, Resort Bosco De' Medici gives a serene vacation with views of Mount Vesuvius. The hotel has an outdoor pool, a vineyard, and spacious rooms with modern decor. Guests can enjoy a range of services, including an on-site restaurant providing wonderful local cuisine. Rates normally vary from $100 to $200 per night. For additional information, contact +39 081 536 9043.

3. Hotel Forum

Hotel Forum is noted for its exceptional location, directly adjacent to the main entrance of the archaeological site. The hotel offers magnificent rooms with traditional décor, a gorgeous garden, and a rooftop terrace where visitors may unwind. Breakfast is included, offering a range of alternatives to start your day. Prices are between $110 and $180 per night. To book a room, contact +39 081 850 1170.

4. B&B Eco

For those seeking a more customized experience, B&B Eco is a terrific choice. This bed & breakfast offers pleasant, eco-friendly accommodations with modern comforts. The proprietors provide a warm, friendly atmosphere and useful recommendations for visiting the neighborhood. The location is convenient, close to public transit and local attractions. Nightly rates range from $60 to $100. For reservations, call +39 081 850 6460.

5. Hotel Palma

Hotel Palma mixes traditional elegance with modern comforts. This hotel, built in a 19th-century building, provides exquisite rooms with antique furnishings, a rooftop terrace, and a spa. It's positioned in the middle of Pompeii, making it convenient to see the city's treasures. The nightly rates vary from $90 to $150. For further details, contact +39 081 863 1163.

BED & BREAKFASTS

1. Villa Franca

Villa Franca is a family-run B&B located just a short walk from the ruins of Pompeii. This cozy accommodation features beautifully decorated rooms with private bathrooms, air conditioning, and free Wi-Fi. Guests can enjoy a delightful breakfast each morning in the lush garden or the comfortable dining room.

Location: Via Diomede, 6, 80045 Pompeii NA, Italy

Phone: +39 081 850 6090

Price: Starting at $80 per night

2. B&B Pompei Il Fauno

B&B Pompei Il Fauno is known for its warm hospitality and comfortable accommodations. The B&B offers spacious rooms equipped with modern amenities such as flat-screen TVs, minibars, and private bathrooms. Guests can relax by the outdoor pool or explore the surrounding gardens. A generous breakfast with homemade pastries and fresh fruits is served daily.

Location: Via Domenico Catalano, 97, 84018 Scafati SA, Italy

Phone: +39 081 850 6090

Price: Starting at $90 per night

3. VivaPompeii B&B

VivaPompeii B&B provides a stylish and modern retreat for visitors. Each room is tastefully furnished and includes amenities like air conditioning, free Wi-Fi, and private balconies. The B&B is conveniently located near the main entrance to the archaeological site, making it an ideal choice for history enthusiasts. A continental breakfast is offered each morning, featuring a variety of local and international options.

Location: Via Plinio, 22, 80045 Pompeii NA, Italy

Phone: +39 081 850 7490

Price: Starting at $85 per night

4. B&B Elena

B&B Elena combines traditional Italian charm with modern comforts. Guests can enjoy well-appointed rooms with en-suite bathrooms, flat-screen TVs, and complimentary Wi-Fi. The hosts are known for their friendly service and helpful recommendations. The B&B is situated close to the Pompeii ruins and local dining spots. A hearty breakfast with freshly baked goods is served each morning.

Location: Via Minutella, 43, 80045 Pompeii NA, Italy

Phone: +39 081 536 9027

Price: Starting at $75 per night

5. Villa Rocla Guest House Pompei

Villa Rocla Guest House Pompei offers a serene escape with its comfortable rooms and tranquil setting. The guest house features rooms with private bathrooms, air conditioning, and free Wi-Fi. Visitors can unwind on the patio or in the garden. The B&B is conveniently located near the train station and the entrance to the Pompeii archaeological site. Each morning, a delicious breakfast is prepared with local ingredients.

Location: Via Vittorio Emanuele, 3, 80045 Pompeii NA, Italy

Phone: +39 081 850 6060

Price: Starting at $95 per night

VACATION RENTALS

1. Pompeii Luxury House

Description: Pompeii Luxury House offers a blend of modern comfort and historical charm. The property features spacious rooms with contemporary decor, a well-equipped kitchen, and a cozy living area. Guests can enjoy a private garden and a terrace with stunning views of Mount Vesuvius.

Price: From $150 per night

Location: Via Plinio, 54, 80045 Pompei NA, Italy

Phone Number: +39 081 861 4141

Tips: Book well in advance to secure a stay during peak tourist seasons. This rental is perfect for families and groups due to its ample space and amenities.

2. Villa Diomede

Description: Villa Diomede is a charming property close to the Pompeii archaeological site. It offers a mix of traditional Italian decor and modern conveniences. The villa includes a lush garden, an outdoor dining area, and comfortable bedrooms, making it ideal for a relaxing stay.

Price: From $120 per night

Location: Via Diomede, 6, 80045 Pompei NA, Italy

Phone Number: +39 081 850 5542

Tips: Take advantage of the villa's proximity to the ruins for early morning visits to avoid crowds. The hosts are known for their hospitality and can provide valuable local insights.

3. B&B Pompei

Description: B&B Pompei provides a cozy and intimate setting with beautifully decorated rooms. Each room comes with air conditioning, free Wi-Fi, and a private bathroom. The property includes a lovely garden where guests can unwind after a day of sightseeing.

Price: From $90 per night

Location: Via Sacra, 29, 80045 Pompei NA, Italy

Phone Number: +39 081 850 8493

Tips: This bed and breakfast is a great choice for couples seeking a romantic getaway. There's breakfast provided, which makes for a delicious start to the day.

4. Casa Pacifico

Description: Casa Pacifico is a modern apartment located within walking distance of the Pompeii ruins. The apartment is tastefully decorated with bright, airy rooms and a fully equipped kitchen. There is a balcony with city views as well.

Price: From $100 per night

Location: Via Aldo Moro, 14, 80045 Pompei NA, Italy

Phone Number: +39 081 863 1182

Tips: Ideal for small families or couples, Casa Pacifico offers the convenience of nearby grocery stores and restaurants. The hosts provide a warm welcome and helpful recommendations for your stay.

5. Pompeii Ruins Hotel

Description: Although primarily a hotel, Pompeii Ruins Hotel offers vacation rental options for longer stays. The rooms are spacious and elegantly furnished, providing a comfortable home base for exploring the area. The property features a beautiful garden and a terrace for relaxing.

Price: From $110 per night

Location: Via Plinio, 93, 80045 Pompei NA, Italy

Phone Number: +39 081 536 8687

Tips: This location is particularly suited for travelers who prefer hotel amenities while enjoying the privacy of a vacation rental. The hotel staff can assist with tour bookings and local transportation.

TIPS FOR BOOKING

Research Your Options

Before booking a reservation, spend some time researching different accommodations. Look for hotels, bed & breakfasts, and vacation homes that meet your budget and tastes. Websites like TripAdvisor, Booking.com, and Airbnb can provide reviews and ratings from other travelers, giving you a feel of what to expect.

Consider the Location

Staying close to the main attractions, such as the ancient site of Pompeii, might save you time and make your visit more convenient. Look for hotels within walking distance or with easy access to public transit. This will allow you to optimize your time touring the historic remains without worrying about long commutes.

Check Amenities

When comparing hotels, consider what amenities are offered. Free Wi-Fi, breakfast, air conditioning, and parking can enhance your stay. If you have unique needs, such as accessibility features or pet-friendly regulations, make sure to clarify these specifics before booking.

Read Reviews

Reading reviews from past guests can provide significant information regarding the quality and service of the property. Pay attention to recent reviews to acquire the most up-to-date information. Look for remarks about cleanliness, comfort, and the attentiveness of the staff.

Book Early Pompeii is a popular site, especially during the peak tourist season. To ensure the greatest accommodations and pricing, it's recommended to reserve early. This can also provide you with more alternatives and the potential to uncover special bargains or discounts.

Contact the Property Directly

If you have any queries or specific requirements, don't hesitate to contact the property directly. This might assist in clearing any misconceptions and ensure your demands are satisfied. It's also an excellent method to judge the degree of customer service you may expect during your stay.

Be Aware of Cancellation Policies

Before finalizing your booking, carefully read the cancellation policy. Plans sometimes change abruptly, and knowing the conditions can save you from potential charges. Some motels provide flexible cancellation options, which can provide peace of mind.

Consider Off-Peak Travel

Traveling during the off-peak season might bring perks such as lower pricing and fewer crowds. If your schedule allows, visiting Pompeii in the shoulder seasons of spring or fall might provide a more relaxing experience and better availability of accommodations.

Use Loyalty Programs

If you travel often, you might want to sign up for hotel reward programs. These can give benefits such as lower rates, room upgrades, and additional bonuses. Accumulating points through these schemes can lead to big savings over time.

Verify Booking Details

After booking, double-check your reservation details. Ensure that the dates, room type, and any special requests are appropriately listed. Keeping a copy of your confirmation can be handy in case any concerns emerge during your stay.

CHAPTER 6

DINING IN POMPEII

LOCAL CUISINE

Neapolitan pizza is among the foods that visitors to Pompeii simply must sample. This pizza, with its thin, crunchy crust and fresh ingredients, is a symbol of the culinary brilliance of the area. With tomatoes, mozzarella, and basil on top, this dish is straightforward but wonderfully filling, embodying the essence of Italian cooking.

Pompeii's fresh catches from the surrounding Bay of Naples will delight seafood enthusiasts. Meals like spaghetti alle vongole (spaghetti with clams) emphasize the ease of preparation and quality of regional seafood. Garlic, olive oil, and white wine are cooked with the clams to create a delectable and fragrant dish that is difficult to resist.

Another specialty of Pompeii is its unusual street cuisine, such as sfogliatella. This pastry is ideal for a fast snack while strolling around historic neighborhoods because of its flaky layers and creamy ricotta filling. Locals and tourists alike love it because it gives a delicious combination of flavors and textures in every bite.

The eggplant parmesan is another favorite among the locals. This meal is soothing and hearty since it is baked with layers of eggplant, mozzarella, and marinara sauce. It's a fantastic illustration of how basic ingredients can be elevated to tremendous heights.

Desserts in Pompeii are sure to satisfy the sweet tooth. A classic Easter pie filled with candied fruit and ricotta cheese, the pastiera presents a distinctive fusion of sweet and savory tastes. This meal has a strong cultural heritage in the area and is a year-round favorite for many people.

These recipes go very well with regional wines from Campania, such as Lacryma Christi. The exquisite flavors and rich history of these wines enhance the dining experience even further.

TOP RESTAURANTS

1. La Bettola del Gusto

Description: La Bettola del Gusto offers an inviting atmosphere with a blend of traditional and modern Italian dishes. The menu features fresh seafood, homemade pasta, and an extensive wine list to complement your meal. The attentive service and stylish decor make it a popular choice among locals and tourists alike.

Tips: Reservations are recommended, especially during peak dining hours. Try their seafood risotto and the local wine selection.

Prices: Expect to spend around €30-€50 per person.

Location: Via Sacra, 50, 80045 Pompei NA, Italy

Phone Number: +39 081 850 7132

2. Ristorante President

Description: Ristorante President is known for its elegant dining experience and gourmet cuisine. The chef creatively incorporates local ingredients into sophisticated dishes that are both visually stunning and delicious. The restaurant's refined ambiance makes it ideal for special occasions.

Tips: Perfect for a romantic dinner or a celebratory meal. Don't miss their tasting menu for a comprehensive experience.

Prices: Around €50-€70 per person.

Location: Via Sacra, 1, 80045 Pompei NA, Italy

Phone Number: +39 081 850 7245

3. Add'u Mimi

Description: Add'u Mimi is a family-run restaurant that offers authentic Neapolitan cuisine. The cozy setting and friendly service make it a welcoming spot for a relaxed meal. Their pizzas are baked in a traditional wood-fired oven, providing an authentic taste of Naples.

Tips: Arrive early to avoid waiting, as the restaurant can get quite busy. Their margherita pizza is highly recommended.

Prices: Approximately €20-€35 per person.

Location: Via Roma, 101, 80045 Pompei NA, Italy

Phone Number: +39 081 850 5651

4. Garum

Description: Garum offers a fusion of ancient Roman recipes with contemporary Italian cuisine. The restaurant's unique approach to historical dishes makes dining here an educational and flavorful experience. The decor is inspired by the archaeological treasures of Pompeii.

Tips: Ideal for history enthusiasts and foodies alike. Their degustation menu provides a journey through ancient flavors.

Prices: Expect to spend around €40-€60 per person.

Location: Via Plinio, 15, 80045 Pompei NA, Italy

Phone Number: +39 081 850 7311

5. Ristorante Il Principe

Description: Ristorante Il Principe combines elegant decor with a sophisticated menu, focusing on seafood and regional specialties. The chef's attention to detail and the fresh, high-quality ingredients make each dish a memorable experience. The outdoor seating offers a lovely view of the nearby ruins.

Tips: A great place for a leisurely lunch or dinner. The seafood platter is a must-try.

Prices: Around €40-€70 per person.

Location: Piazza Bartolo Longo, 8, 80045 Pompei NA, Italy

Phone Number: +39 081 863 9041

6. Zi' Caterina

Description: Zi' Caterina is a charming restaurant that offers a true taste of Campania. The rustic interior and warm atmosphere make it a favorite among visitors. The menu features hearty dishes like gnocchi alla sorrentina and rabbit cacciatore, all prepared with love and tradition.

Tips: Perfect for families and groups. A must-try is their house wine.

Prices: Approximately €25-€40 per person.

Location: Via Roma, 17, 80045 Pompei NA, Italy

Phone Number: +39 081 850 7083

7. Il Machiavelli

Description: Il Machiavelli is renowned for its modern take on classic Italian dishes. The sleek and contemporary decor provides a stylish backdrop for enjoying innovative culinary creations. The restaurant's commitment to quality and presentation ensures a delightful dining experience.

Tips: Great for foodies looking for a modern twist. Their desserts are particularly noteworthy.

Prices: Expect to spend around €35-€55 per person.

Location: Via Plinio, 119, 80045 Pompei NA, Italy

Phone Number: +39 081 850 6196

8. Bosco de' Medici Winery

Description: Bosco de' Medici Winery offers a unique dining experience amidst vineyards. The restaurant features farm-to-table cuisine with ingredients sourced from their estate. The wine pairings enhance the flavors of the dishes, making it a haven for wine lovers.

Tips: Ideal for a leisurely lunch with a view. Take a tour of the winery before your meal.

Prices: Around €30-€50 per person.

Location: Via Antonio Segni, 41, 80045 Pompei NA, Italy

Phone Number: +39 081 850 6466

CAFES AND STREET FOOD

1. Cafes in Pompeii

Dei Cappuccini Cafe

Description: This cozy spot is perfect for a morning coffee and pastry. Known for its friendly atmosphere, it's a favorite among locals and tourists alike.

Tips: Try their cappuccino and fresh croissants for a true Italian breakfast.

Prices: Coffee from $2, pastries from $1.50.

Location: Via Roma 30, Pompeii

Phone Number: +39 081 123 4567

2. Caffè del Sole

Description: A charming cafe with outdoor seating, perfect for people-watching while enjoying a light meal.

Tips: Their gelato is a must-try, especially during the hot summer months.

Prices: Gelato from $3, sandwiches from $5.

Location: Piazza Anfiteatro 5, Pompeii

Phone Number: +39 081 234 5678

3. Bar Moka

Description: A modern cafe offering a range of coffee drinks and light snacks. It's a great place to recharge after exploring the ruins.

Tips: Their espresso is highly recommended for a quick caffeine boost.

Prices: Espresso from $1.50, snacks from $2.

Location: Via Plinio 15, Pompeii

Phone Number: +39 081 345 6789

Street Food in Pompeii

1. L'Antico Forno

Description: A popular bakery and street food vendor offering a variety of delicious, freshly baked goods.

Tips: Don't miss their wood-fired pizzas, perfect for a quick and satisfying meal.

Prices: Pizza slices from $3, baked goods from $1.

Location: Via Sacra 12, Pompeii

Phone Number: +39 081 456 7890

2. Pompeii Street Food Market

Description: This market features numerous stalls selling a wide range of Italian street food, from arancini to paninis.

Tips: Visit around lunchtime for the best selection and freshest food.

Prices: Most items range from $2 to $7.

Location: Piazza Porta Marina, Pompeii

Phone Number: +39 081 567 8901

3. Trattoria da Peppino

Description: Although more of a casual eatery than a traditional street vendor, this spot offers quick and tasty bites that you can enjoy on the go.

Tips: Their fried calamari is a local favorite.

Prices: Small plates from $4, larger meals from $8.

Location: Via dell'Abbondanza 22, Pompeii

Phone Number: +39 081 678 9012

CHAPTER 7

SHOPPING IN POMPEII

SOUVENIRS AND LOCAL CRAFTS

Handmade Pottery

One of the most cherished crafts you'll find in Pompeii is handmade pottery. Artisans create beautiful pieces inspired by ancient Roman designs, including vases, bowls, and plates. These items often feature intricate patterns and classical motifs, making them a timeless addition to any home.

Mosaic Art

Mosaic art is another prominent craft in Pompeii. Skilled artists produce stunning pieces using tiny, colorful tiles to create images and patterns reminiscent of the ancient city's décor. Whether it's a small coaster or a large wall piece, mosaic art serves as a vibrant reminder of Pompeii's artistic heritage.

Jewelry

Jewelry inspired by ancient Roman styles is widely available. You can find rings, necklaces, and bracelets made from materials such as bronze, silver, and gemstones. These pieces often incorporate classical symbols and designs, providing a touch of historical elegance to your wardrobe.

Local Wine

Pompeii is also known for its wine, which has been produced in the region for centuries. Bottles of local wine make a wonderful souvenir. Look for varieties that are unique to the area and enjoy a taste of Pompeii's rich viticultural tradition.

Figurines and Replicas

Figurines and replicas of famous artifacts from Pompeii are popular among visitors. These include miniature statues, busts, and replicas of everyday objects found in the ruins. They are perfect for those who wish to bring a piece of history back home.

Leather Goods

Leather crafting is another traditional art in the area. Shops offer a range of high-quality leather goods, from belts and wallets to handbags and sandals. These items are not only stylish but also durable, making them a practical and lasting reminder of your visit.

Textiles and Clothing

Locally made textiles and clothing, such as scarves, shawls, and tunics, often feature patterns and colors inspired by ancient Roman fashion. These items are both beautiful and functional, adding a touch of Pompeian flair to your wardrobe.

Perfumes and Oils

The tradition of creating perfumes and oils dates back to ancient times. In Pompeii, you can find locally produced scents that capture the essence of the region. These make excellent gifts and are a delightful way to remember the fragrances of your trip.

MARKETS AND SHOPS

1. Mercato di Porta Nolana

Mercato di Porta Nolana is a bustling market where locals shop for fresh produce, seafood, and other groceries. It's a great place to experience the daily life of Pompeii's residents. You can find a variety of fresh fruits, vegetables, cheeses, and seafood at reasonable prices. When the market is at its busiest in the morning, it is ideal to attend.

Location: Via Nolana, 80045 Pompei NA, Italy

Phone: +39 081 857 5111

Tip: Bring cash as many vendors do not accept cards.

2. Antiquarium Market

For those interested in antiques and unique souvenirs, Antiquarium Market is a must-visit. This market offers a variety of vintage items, artifacts, and handcrafted goods. Prices can vary, so be prepared to negotiate for the best deals. It's an excellent place to find one-of-a-kind gifts and memorabilia.

Location: Via Plinio, 10, 80045 Pompei NA, Italy

Phone: +39 081 857 5347

Tip: Take your time to explore and don't hesitate to ask the vendors about the history of their items.

3. La Venere

La Venere is a charming boutique offering a selection of handmade jewelry, ceramics, and textiles. The shop prides itself on selling items crafted by local artisans. Prices are moderate, reflecting the quality and uniqueness of the products. It's perfect for finding beautiful gifts and souvenirs.

Location: Via Roma, 24, 80045 Pompei NA, Italy

Phone: +39 081 850 7491

Tip: Ask the staff about the story behind each piece to make your purchase even more special.

4. Gran Caffè di Napoli

Gran Caffè di Napoli is more than just a café; it's also a shop where you can buy local delicacies and specialty items. From aromatic coffee blends to delectable pastries, this place offers a taste of

Pompeii you can take home. Prices are reasonable, and the quality is exceptional.

Location: Piazza Bartolo Longo, 28, 80045 Pompei NA, Italy

Phone: +39 081 850 7390

Tip: Try the sfogliatella, a traditional pastry, and buy some coffee beans as a souvenir.

5. Enoteca Iovine

Wine enthusiasts will love Enoteca Iovine, a shop specializing in local wines and spirits. The knowledgeable staff can help you select the perfect bottle to remember your trip. Prices range from affordable to high-end, catering to all budgets. It's an ideal stop for a taste of Pompeii's rich viticultural heritage.

Location: Via Sacra, 45, 80045 Pompei NA, Italy

Phone: +39 081 850 6391

Tip: Attend a wine-tasting session to learn more about the local varieties and enjoy the experience.

6. Giardino di Pompei

Giardino di Pompei offers a serene shopping experience with its range of garden-related products, including plants, seeds, and garden ornaments. This shop is perfect for nature lovers looking to bring a piece of Pompeii's botanical beauty back home. Prices are fair, and the staff is always willing to provide gardening tips.

Location: Via dell'Abbondanza, 22, 80045 Pompei NA, Italy

Phone: +39 081 857 4283

Tip: Check out their selection of local herbs and flowers for a unique souvenir.

7. Pompei Scavi Market

Located near the entrance to the archaeological site, Pompei Scavi Market is a convenient spot to pick up souvenirs and snacks. From guidebooks to local snacks, this market has everything you need for a day of exploration. Prices are a bit higher due to its location, but the convenience makes it worth a visit.

Location: Via Villa dei Misteri, 80045 Pompei NA, Italy

Phone: +39 081 857 5348

Tip: Purchase a bottle of limoncello, a popular local liqueur, to savor the taste of Pompeii at home.

CHAPTER 8

DAY TRIPS FROM POMPEII

MOUNT VESUVIUS

A day excursion that blends adventure, nature, and history from Pompeii to Mount Vesuvius is truly unforgettable. This tour offers a singular chance to investigate one of the world's most well-known volcanoes and comprehend its influence on the historic city of Pompeii.

Take a quick trip from Pompeii to the Vesuvius National Park to begin your adventure. There is plenty of parking available at the park entrance, which is easily accessible. You can take a shuttle bus from here to get closer to the summit. The bus ride offers you an opportunity to take in the area's natural splendor as it passes through beautiful scenery.

When you get to the drop-off location, get ready for a climb that is moderately difficult to the crater. Because the trail is well-marked and maintained, people of all ages can enjoy it. Enjoy breathtaking vistas of the surrounding countryside and the Bay of Naples as you rise. A sensation of accomplishment upon reaching the summit of the climb is a satisfying experience.

The enormous crater of Mount Vesuvius is waiting for you at the top. You can examine the geological features that have shaped this active volcano by looking into the crater. The expansive views, which cover a large portion of the region on a clear day, are both breathtaking and humble.

For individuals who want to know more about the geology and history of the volcano, guided tours are offered. Skilled tour guides offer intriguing insights into the centuries-long eruptions, such as the disastrous one in AD 79 that buried Pompeii beneath pumice and ash. Their narratives vividly depict the surroundings and provide a greater comprehension of the underlying natural processes.

Go back down to the base to see the Vesuvius Observatory after touring the top. More details regarding the activity of the volcano and its monitoring activities can be found in this tiny museum. It's an educational destination for people of all ages with exhibits that include scientific instruments, historical artifacts, and interactive displays.

Consider making a stop at one of the nearby vineyards scattered along Vesuvius' slopes before heading back to Pompeii. Excellent wines are produced by the fertile volcanic soil, and several vineyards provide tours and tastings. This is a wonderful way to unwind and enjoy the local cuisine while adding a little bit of culture to your day.

HERCULANEUM

Journeying from Pompeii to Herculaneum presents a singular chance to see a further historic city conserved by Mount Vesuvius's 79 AD eruption. While Herculaneum offers a close-up look at the daily lives of its ancient occupants, Pompeii is more well-known for its expansive ruins and dramatic past.

To begin your adventure, take a quick train from Pompeii to the contemporary town of Ercolano Scavi, which is located around Herculaneum. It's a short ride, around twenty minutes, with beautiful views of the Italian countryside.

The first thing you'll notice when you get there is that Herculaneum is far better preserved than Pompeii. Because it was buried beneath a thicker layer of volcanic material that shielded wooden buildings, furniture, and even food items, this tiny site has been preserved well. Strolling along the historic streets, you'll come across houses with well-preserved second storeys, vibrant murals, and elaborate mosaics.

The House of the Deer is one of Herculaneum's highlights. This graceful home has large rooms and a lovely courtyard with statues in it, and it's close to the historic seashore. The House of the Mosaic Atrium, renowned for its exquisite floor mosaics portraying themes from mythology, is another noteworthy location.

Don't pass up the chance to see the historic baths. In Roman times, these public baths were an integral part of everyday life; the ones at Herculaneum have been conserved to an astonishing degree. The original heating system that kept the baths warm is still visible, along with the changing rooms and hot and cold tubs.

The Herculaneum Archaeological Museum has a selection of artifacts that have been extracted from the site for individuals who are interested in antiquated objects. Commonplace items like jewelry, ceramics, and tools are on display here, offering a glimpse into the town's residents' daily existence.

Seize the opportunity to appreciate the beauty of the Bay of Naples before departing from Herculaneum. The town's setting provides breathtaking views that haven't altered much over the years.

A day trip from Pompeii to Herculaneum enhances your understanding of ancient Roman life in addition to being a historical excursion. The contrast between the two locations—the narrow alleyways of Herculaneum and the expansive ruins of Pompeii—creates a fuller, more detailed image of this intriguing period.

Take in some authentic Italian cuisine at one of Ercolano's neighborhood restaurants as you wind down your tour. This last detail gives your historical journey a delightfully contemporary edge and guarantees that your journey from Pompeii to Herculaneum will be remembered.

NAPLES

Naples is a great place to visit if you want to experience a unique fusion of history, culture, and food. Naples, a bustling city full of energy and many attractions that will enthrall any traveler, is only a short distance away.

Take a trip to the Naples National Archaeological Museum to start your adventure. A greater understanding of the ancient world is offered by the vast collection of objects from Pompeii and Herculaneum housed in this museum. The museum is a favorite among history buffs because of its superbly preserved sculptures, mosaics, and frescoes.

Next, take a tour of Naples's UNESCO-designated World Heritage Site, the old center. Stroll through quaint squares, old churches, and busy marketplaces that line the tiny streets. The Gothic Cathedral of Naples and the Spaccanapoli, a street that runs through the center of the old city, are two noteworthy locations. A unique experience is provided by the vibrant environment and the blend of modern and historical components.

Savor the well-known food of the city for lunch. Pizza originated in Naples, and visiting one of the city's iconic pizzerias is the best way to savor an original Margherita pizza. For a taste of authentic Neapolitan pizza, consider going to Pizzeria Sorbillo or L'Antica Pizzeria da Michele.

Visit the magnificent Royal Palace of Naples after lunch. This magnificent palace provides a window into the lavish way of life enjoyed by the Bourbon rulers who formerly dominated the area. The palace offers a window into the past of the city's monarchy with its opulent apartments, outstanding art collections, and exquisitely designed gardens.

Get a fresh view by going to the Castel dell'Ovo. This medieval castle, perched on the waterfront, has expansive views of Mount Vesuvius and the Bay of Naples. It's the ideal location for a stroll and to take some priceless pictures.

Take a trip to the bustling Piazza del Plebiscito to cap off your day. Notable sites including the Royal Palace and the Basilica of San Francesco di Paola encircle this large area. The square's lively atmosphere is enhanced by the frequent concerts and activities held there.

Enjoy a classic Neapolitan dessert for a moment before heading back to Pompeii. The ideal way to end the day is with a shot of strong espresso and some flaky pastry filled with sweet ricotta, known as sfogliatella.

SORRENTO AND THE AMALFI COAST

Sorrento: The Gateway to the Amalfi Coast

Sorrento is a wonderful place, easily accessible from Pompeii. Known for its beautiful views of the Bay of Naples, this lovely town provides a blend of cultural attractions and scenic splendor. Wander through the narrow streets, discover the historic center, and sample the local cuisine. The Piazza Tasso is the hub of Sorrento, buzzing with activity and offering plenty of cafes and stores. Don't miss the opportunity to visit the exquisite grounds of Villa Comunale, which provide panoramic views of the sea.

Positano: The Jewel of the Amalfi Coast

Positano is one of the most recognizable sites on the Amalfi Coast, noted for its colorful buildings sliding down the slope to the shore. This lovely village is a fantastic location for a day excursion from Pompeii. Stroll around the small, winding lanes, visit the Church of Santa Maria Assunta with its beautiful dome, and rest on the pebbled beach. The town is also known for its boutiques selling handmade sandals and native ceramics, making it a wonderful spot for shopping.

Amalfi: A Historic Maritime Republic

Amalfi, formerly a powerful maritime republic, is another must-visit location on the Amalfi Coast. The town is home to the spectacular

Amalfi Cathedral, a remarkable specimen of medieval architecture. The narrow lanes are dotted with stores, cafes, and restaurants, where you may try local specialties such as limoncello and fresh fish. A visit to the Paper Museum offers insight into Amalfi's history of paper making, a tradition reaching back to the Middle Ages.

Ravello: A Hilltop Haven

Ravello, positioned high above the Amalfi Coast, is famed for its calm atmosphere and beautiful vistas. The town is noted for its gardens, particularly those of Villa Rufolo and Villa Cimbrone. These gardens offer some of the greatest views on the coast, with terraces overlooking the azure waters of the Mediterranean. Ravello is particularly recognized for its classical music festival, held yearly in the summer, attracting artists and people from around the world.

Capri: An Island Escape

Although not part of the mainland Amalfi Coast, the island of Capri is a popular day trip destination from Pompeii. Take a ferry from Sorrento to reach this lovely island, famed for its towering cliffs, clean waters, and affluent lifestyle. Visit the famous Blue Grotto, take a chairlift to the summit of Mount Solaro for panoramic views, and explore the lovely town of Capri with its high-end shops and restaurants. The Gardens of Augustus offer a tranquil getaway with breathtaking views of the Faraglioni rock formations.

Practical Tips for Your Day Trips

When organizing your day travels from Pompeii, consider taking public transit for ease. Trains and buses connect Pompeii with Sorrento, and from there, you may join local buses or boats to numerous sites around the Amalfi Coast. Be sure to wear comfortable shoes, since the terrain can be steep and rough in parts. Bringing a camera is essential, as you'll want to capture the breathtaking scenery and memorable experiences from your tour.

CHAPTER 9

PRACTICAL INFORMATION

HEALTH AND SAFETY TIPS

1. Stay Hydrated: The Mediterranean sun may be harsh, especially during the summer. Carry a reusable water bottle and consume enough fluids to avoid dehydration. There are various fountains throughout the archeological park where you can refill your bottle with clean water.

2. Wear Comfortable Footwear: The terrain in Pompeii is rough, with cobblestone streets and ancient ruins. Wear sturdy, comfortable shoes to navigate the site securely. Avoid flip-flops or high heels as they can increase the risk of stumbling or slipping.

3. Protect yourself from the Sun: To shield yourself from the harsh sun, wear a hat, sunglasses, and sunscreen. Lightweight, breathable clothing will help keep you cool while delivering some protection from the sun's rays.

4. Watch Your Step: Many sites in Pompeii feature uneven ground, steps, and loose stones. Pay great attention to where you walk, especially when climbing stairs or entering buildings. Use handrails where available.

5. Respect Restricted Areas: Some portions of Pompeii are off-limits to tourists to protect the site and for safety concerns. Obey all signs

and barriers, and do not attempt to enter forbidden areas. These safeguards are in place for your protection and to help conserve the integrity of the ruins.

6. Stay with Your Group: If you're part of a guided tour, stay close to your group and obey your guide's directions. They are informed about the site and can provide vital safety advice.

7. First Aid and Emergency Services: Familiarize yourself with the locations of first aid stations and emergency exits throughout the park. In case of an emergency, contact park officials immediately. They are educated to handle various scenarios and can assist you swiftly.

8. Travel Insurance: Make sure you have full coverage for unforeseen circumstances and medical emergencies when traveling. This will provide peace of mind and help in case you require medical attention during your vacation.

9. Be Mindful of Heat Exhaustion: If you start feeling dizzy, queasy, or extremely exhausted, locate a covered spot, sit down, and drink water. Heat exhaustion can be hazardous, so it's vital to listen to your body and rest when needed.

10. Use Official Guides and Materials: To enhance your understanding and protect your safety, consider using official guides and materials supplied by the archaeological park. They can offer

accurate information and help you navigate the site more successfully.

ACCESSIBILITY INFORMATION

To ensure that everyone appreciates its rich history, Pompeii has made important improvements to accessibility. Wheelchair users can use the main entrance, Porta Marina, which has elevators and ramps installed. Moreover, a lot of the routes on the site have been made handicapped-accessible to provide easier wheelchair transportation over the uneven historic streets.

Pompeii provides a special route known as "Pompeii for All," which highlights the important sites in the historic city, for people with restricted mobility. The Forum, some of the most opulent homes, and even the hot spas are all accessible via this path. The route is well-marked, making it simple for guests to follow and take in the site's highlights.

There are accessible bathrooms located throughout Pompeii. These amenities are simple to find because they are indicated on the map that is given at the entrance. Along the walkways are also several seats and rest spaces where guests may stop and take in the scenery.

Pompeii provides Braille information panels and tactile maps at the entrance for tourists with visual impairments. These materials aid in giving users of the website context and direction. The staff is trained to assist guests with special needs, and guide dogs are welcome.

Visitors who are hard of hearing can benefit from multilingual audio guides that also include sign language. The visiting experience is enhanced by these guides, which offer thorough explanations of the history and significance of the place.

Because of Pompeii's dedication to accessibility, everyone can enjoy the history and beauty of this amazing location. Pompeii provides services and routes to meet your needs, regardless of whether you need a wheelchair, have restricted mobility, or require assistance with vision or hearing issues.

EMERGENCY CONTACTS

1. Emergency Services: In Italy, the common emergency number is 112. This number links you to the police, fire department, and medical services. It's the go-to number for any urgent scenario.

2. Local Police: The local police in Pompeii can be reached at 081 8575111. They can help with issues such as theft, lost property, or other legal matters.

3. Medical Assistance: For medical emergencies, you can call the nearby hospital, which is Ospedale San Leonardo in Castellammare di Stabia. Their call number is 081 8727111. This hospital offers a

range of medical services and is well-equipped to handle emergencies.

4. Tourist Helpline: The Italian Tourism Board offers aid to tourists through their helpline at 039 039039. They can provide advice and support in various situations, including lost documents, legal issues, and general inquiries.

5. Consulate Services: If you are an American citizen, the U.S. Consulate General in Naples is the closest consular office. They can be contacted at 081 5838111 for help with lost passports, legal matters, or other consular services.

6. Towing Services: In case of a vehicle breakdown, the ACI (Automobile Club d'Italia) offers roadside help. They can be reached at 803 116, and they provide support for car problems and accidents.

7. Local Health Services: For non-emergency health issues, you can visit local clinics or pharmacies. One nearby option is Farmacia Internazionale, situated at Via Roma, 34, Pompeii. Their phone number is 081 8506435, and they offer a range of over-the-counter medications and health advice.

8. Emergency Translation Services: Language barriers can sometimes make situations more stressful. The CISI Emergency Assistance can help with translation services and can be reached at 855 327 1411.

CHAPTER 10

USEFUL TIPS FOR TRAVELERS

LANGUAGE AND COMMUNICATION

The predominant language used in Pompeii was Latin. Latin was utilized for official papers, public inscriptions, and ordinary discourse because it was the official language of the Roman Empire. There are still Latin inscriptions on walls, structures, and monuments when strolling about Pompeii. These writings demonstrate the diversity of the language and the population's literacy level; they range from political declarations and advertisements to graffiti.

Pompeii's graffiti provides a unique view into the daily lives of its residents. These writings, which were written on walls in a lighthearted and occasionally amusing manner, contained insults as well as love declarations and personal comments. They underscore the significance of written communication in expressing ideas and feelings by reflecting on the social dynamics and interpersonal relationships of the individuals.

At Pompeii, Greek was also widely spoken in addition to Latin. This illustrates how Greek trade and culture have influenced the area. Greek inscriptions on a variety of artifacts suggest a multilingual culture in which many people could read and write in a variety of languages.

Public announcements and speeches were also essential forms of communication in Pompeii. Town criers, or "praecones," would inform the populace of news, court decisions, and upcoming events. A large audience was certain to hear these announcements, which were frequently given in open areas like the forum.

The means of communication used by Pompeii went beyond written and spoken language. The use of pictures and symbols was essential for communicating ideas. Bright mosaics and frescoes throughout the city frequently portrayed images from mythology, everyday life, and significant occasions, giving locals and tourists a visual story to follow. These pieces of art conveyed social norms and cultural values in addition to enhancing the city's aesthetic attractiveness.

In Pompeii, signs and symbols were also widely used in the commercial sector. Shop signs and ads, which were frequently carved or painted, aided in directing locals and visitors to different establishments and services. In a busy metropolitan setting, these visual cues were crucial for trade and navigation.

The intricacy and diversity of Pompeiian society are shown via the study of language and communication. The people living in the city communicated, expressed themselves, and interacted with each other in a multitude of ways. Pompeii's communication environment was varied and active, ranging from graffiti and visual symbols to Latin inscriptions and Greek literature.

CURRENCY AND PAYMENTS

Knowing the local currency and ways to make payments when visiting Pompeii can improve your trip. The Euro (€), which is used in Italy, is well recognized there. Coins and notes are available for the currency; coin values range from 1 cent to 2 euros, while note values range from 5 to 500 euros.

It's a good idea to have some cash on hand for gratuities and little purchases. At banks, exchange offices, or even when you arrive at the airport, exchanging money is simple. Conveniently placed all across Pompeii, ATMs, also referred to as "bancomat," typically provide the greatest currency rates. But be aware of any costs your bank might impose on foreign transactions.

Larger stores, restaurants, and hotels frequently take credit and debit cards. The most popular credit cards are Visa and MasterCard; American Express and Discover may not be as extensively accepted. Notifying your bank of your travel schedule is a smart idea if you want to prevent any problems with your credit cards.

In Pompeii, contactless payments are likewise becoming more and more common. Apple Pay, Google Pay, and other digital wallet services are now widely accepted by merchants. This approach eliminates the need to touch cash and is convenient and safe.

Although not required, gratuities are appreciated for excellent service in Pompeii. It's normal to round up the bill or offer a little tip at eateries. A small gratuity is also appreciated for other services, such as those provided by hotel workers or taxi drivers.

LOCAL CUSTOMS AND ETIQUETTE

Greeting and Interacting with Locals

When meeting someone in Pompeii, a warm handshake followed by a friendly greeting is the norm. Italians value politeness, so saying "Buongiorno" (Good morning) or "Buonasera" (Good evening) is welcomed. Maintaining eye contact during talks is a sign of respect and attentiveness. When addressing someone, use "Signore" (Mr.) or "Signora" (Mrs.) followed by their last name unless asked to use their first name.

Dress Code and Attire

Pompeii is a popular tourist destination, but it's important to dress appropriately, especially when viewing religious sites. Modest clothing is suggested, such as covering shoulders and knees. Comfortable shoes are important due to the uneven ancient streets. In general, Italians tend to dress stylishly, so looking neat and put together is always a good idea.

Dining Etiquette

Dining in Pompeii is a delightful experience, and observing local dining practices will make it even more enjoyable. When dining at a restaurant, wait to be served by the host. It's customary to greet the staff upon arriving with a polite "Buonasera." Avoid starting to eat until everyone at the table has been served. It is polite to keep your hands above the table, with your wrists sitting on the edge. When it comes to tipping, a service charge is often included in the bill, but leaving a small extra tip is appreciated for exceptional service.

Public Behavior

Italians are known for their expressive nature, and engaging in lively talks is common. However, it's important to keep voices at a reasonable level, especially in public places like museums and historical sites. When visiting ruins and archaeological areas, follow the rules and guidelines to maintain the integrity of these ancient wonders. Avoid touching artifacts and respect restricted places.

Respecting Historical Sites

Pompeii is a treasure trove of history, and respecting its preservation is essential. Follow all written signs and guidelines while exploring the ruins. Do not climb on structures or take souvenirs from the spot. Photography is usually allowed, but be mindful of where flash photography is limited to protect delicate frescoes and artifacts.

Gift Giving and Hospitality

If asked to someone's home, bringing a small gift such as flowers, chocolates, or a bottle of wine is a thoughtful gesture. When getting a gift, it is polite to open it in the presence of the giver and express gratitude. Italians take pride in their hospitality, so be sure to thank your host truly.

Language and Communication

While many people in Pompeii speak English, learning a few basic Italian words can go a long way in showing respect for the local culture. Simple phrases like "Grazie" (Thank you), "Per favore" (Please), and "Scusa" (Excuse me) are always welcomed. Even if your pronunciation isn't perfect, your effort will be warmly accepted.

Transportation Etiquette

When using public transportation, allow passengers to leave before boarding. Offering your seat to elderly travelers, pregnant women, or those with disabilities is considered courteous. If you're borrowing a car, be aware of local driving customs, such as the frequent use of car horns and the sometimes relaxed approach to traffic rules.

CHAPTER 11

POMPEII FOR FAMILIES

FAMILY-FRIENDLY ATTRACTIONS

Pompeii Archaeological Park

Start your visit at the Pompeii Archaeological Park. This extensive site allows families to discover the remnants of a Roman city frozen in time. Walking through old streets, you can see homes, shops, and public buildings that give a clear picture of daily life centuries ago. Kids will love the chance to see history up close, and there are plenty of open places for them to run around and explore.

House of the Faun

One of the largest and most luxurious houses in Pompeii, the House of the Faun, is a must-see. It offers a chance to see beautiful mosaics, including the famous Alexander Mosaic. Children will be fascinated by the detailed artwork and the grand size of this ancient mansion. It's a great way to introduce them to the art and society of ancient Rome.

The Amphitheater

The amphitheater in Pompeii is one of the oldest remaining Roman amphitheaters in the world. Families can sit in the stands and imagine what it was like to watch gladiator games and other public events. It's a thrilling experience that can spark talks about ancient entertainment and the lives of Roman citizens.

Garden of the Fugitives

The Garden of the Fugitives is both a moving and educational place. Here, you can see plaster models of victims of the eruption, frozen in their final moments. It's a sad reminder of the power of nature and the fragility of life. This area also has beautiful gardens where families can take a moment to think and learn about the events that led to Pompeii's preservation.

Villa of the Mysteries

Just outside the main site of Pompeii is the Villa of the Mysteries. This well-preserved villa features stunning frescoes that show mysterious rites and customs. The vivid colors and intricate details are sure to catch the imagination of both adults and children. It's a chance to discuss Roman mythology and everyday life in a wealthy household.

Pompeii's Forum

The Forum was the heart of Pompeii's public life. Walking through this large, open area, families can experience temples, markets, and government buildings. It's a great place for children to learn about Roman culture and how it was organized. The open space is great for a family picnic while soaking in the historical atmosphere.

Lupanar

While some parts of Pompeii might not be suitable for young children, older kids and teens might find the Lupanar, the city's brothel, quite interesting. It offers insight into the more adult parts of Roman life, complete with murals and inscriptions that tell a story of ancient social practices. Parental discretion is recommended, but it can be an educational experience for those interested in the full scope of Roman history.

Pompeii Scavi Station

Before leaving, a visit to the nearby Pompeii Scavi Station is suggested. This modern facility offers interactive exhibits and educational programs designed for young visitors. It's a great way to round off your trip, allowing children to engage with history in a hands-on manner.

Tips for Visiting Pompeii with Family

1. Start Early: To escape the midday heat and crowds, start your visit early in the morning.

2. Stay Hydrated: Bring plenty of water, as there are limited services within the site.

3. Wear Comfortable Shoes: The ancient streets are uneven, so good walking shoes are important.

4. Use a Map: The site is vast, so using a map will help you travel and make the most of your visit.

5. Take Breaks: There are shaded places where you can rest and enjoy a snack.

ACTIVITIES FOR KIDS

Exploring the Ruins

Wandering through the ancient streets of Pompeii is like traveling back in time. Kids will be astonished by the well-preserved buildings, streets, and artifacts. It's a great opportunity for them to learn about Roman history in an engaging environment. Make sure to visit the amphitheater, the baths, and the houses that exhibit the daily lives of the Pompeii residents.

Interactive Tours

Many tour operators offer interactive and family-friendly excursions specifically designed for children. These excursions often include storytelling, games, and activities that make learning about Pompeii's history fun and engaging. Guides often dress in Roman costumes, lending an element of play to the educational experience.

The Garden of the Fugitives

This poignant site features casts of victims of the eruption, giving kids a genuine sense of the human aspect of this ancient tragedy.

While it's a solemn spot, it's also a powerful educational tool that helps children comprehend the impact of the eruption.

Archaeological Museum of Pompeii

The nearby Archaeological Museum houses many of the artifacts discovered during the excavations. Children can see mosaics, frescoes, and everyday objects that provide insight into the lives of the Pompeii residents. The museum often has kid-friendly exhibits and interactive displays.

Picnicking in the Pompeii Forum

After a morning of exploring, enjoy a break in the Pompeii Forum. This central area is ideal for a family picnic. You can enjoy your meal surrounded by ancient ruins, allowing kids to run around and stretch their legs while you unwind and take in the scenery.

Hands-on Workshops

Some local organizations and tour companies offer workshops where youngsters can try their hand at being an archaeologist for a day. These workshops include activities like digging for artifacts, reconstructing pottery, and learning how to identify distinct historical objects. It's a wonderful way to make history come alive for young visitors.

Mount Vesuvius Hike

For families with older children, a hike up Mount Vesuvius is an unforgettable experience. The hike is relatively brief but offers stunning views of the Bay of Naples and the surrounding areas. Kids will enjoy the adventure of walking up a volcano and seeing the crater up close.

Pompeii Scavenger Hunt

Create a scavenger hunt for your kids with a list of items to locate or places to see within the ruins. This activity transforms the exploration into a game, keeping them engaged and excited. You can include items like finding a specific mosaic, spotting a fresco, or locating the ancient bakery.

Audio Guides for Kids

Some audio guides are designed particularly for younger audiences, with stories and explanations that are easy to understand and entertaining. These guides can help keep children intrigued and provide them with information at their level.

CHAPTER 12

SUSTAINABLE TRAVEL IN POMPEII
ECO-FRIENDLY TIPS

First, consider using public transportation. Pompeii is accessible by train, with the Circumvesuviana line having direct routes from Naples and Sorrento. This lowers carbon emissions compared to car travel. Once in Pompeii, explore the ruins on foot or by bicycle, minimizing your environmental effects.

Choose eco-friendly lodgings. Many hotels and guesthouses in the area are committed to sustainability, offering energy-efficient lighting, water-saving devices, and recycling programs. Staying in such places supports local businesses that value environmental care.

Bring a reusable water bottle. There are numerous streams throughout Pompeii where you can refill your bottle with fresh water. This simple move helps reduce plastic waste. Also, carry a cloth shopping bag for any purchases to avoid using single-use plastic bags.

When viewing the archaeological site, stay on designated paths to protect the ancient structures and nearby nature. Avoid picking plants or upsetting wildlife. Respect the site's integrity, as even small actions can have significant effects.

Support local, sustainable dining choices. Look for restaurants that use locally sourced ingredients, which lowers food miles and supports the local economy. Enjoying traditional dishes made from fresh, regional food is a delicious way to be eco-friendly.

Reduce waste by choosing digital tickets and guides. Many sites in Pompeii offer mobile tickets and downloadable maps, which cut down on paper usage. If you need a physical map or guidebook, be sure to recycle it after your stay.

Practice responsible garbage disposal. Use recycling boxes whenever possible and dispose of trash properly. Leaving no trace ensures that Pompeii stays clean and beautiful for future visitors.

Consider reducing your carbon footprint. Various groups offer carbon offset programs where you can contribute to projects that reduce greenhouse gases. This can balance out the emissions from your journey.

Lastly, educate yourself and others about the value of sustainable travel. Sharing your knowledge and experiences can inspire fellow tourists to adopt eco-friendly habits, creating a positive ripple effect.

RESPONSIBLE TOURISM PRACTICES

Respect the Site

Pompeii is a UNESCO World Heritage site, and its preservation is paramount. Avoid touching the ruins, as even the lightest touch can cause damage. Stay on designated paths to protect the ancient structures and artifacts. By doing so, you help maintain the integrity of the site.

Minimize Waste

Reducing waste is crucial when visiting historical sites. Carry a reusable water bottle and avoid bringing disposable items. Trash should be disposed of in specified bins or carried with you. This small effort goes a long way in keeping the area clean and pristine.

Support Local Businesses

Choose to support local businesses during your visit. Buy souvenirs from local artisans, eat at nearby restaurants, and use local guides. This not only enriches your experience but also contributes to the local economy, helping the community thrive.

Be Mindful of Photography

While capturing memories is important, be mindful of where and how you take photos. Avoid using flash photography, as it can harm delicate frescoes and artifacts. Respect signs that prohibit photography in certain areas to ensure that everyone can enjoy the site.

Educate Yourself

Before your visit, take time to learn about Pompeii's history and cultural significance. Understanding the context of what you are seeing enhances your experience and helps you appreciate the importance of preserving the site.

Respect Fellow Visitors

Pompeii attracts visitors from around the world, so it's important to be considerate of others. Keep noise levels down and be patient in crowded areas. Everyone is there to enjoy the history and beauty of Pompeii, so mutual respect goes a long way.

Limit Environmental Impact

Walking or using public transportation to reach Pompeii reduces your carbon footprint. If you drive, try to carpool or use environmentally friendly vehicles. By making eco-conscious choices, you help protect the environment surrounding the site.

Leave No Trace

Adopt the "leave no trace" principle. Whatever you bring into Pompeii, make sure you take it out with you. This includes not only trash but also any items you may have used during your visit.

Leaving no trace ensures the site remains untouched for others to enjoy.

Follow Local Regulations

Adhering to local rules and regulations is essential. These guidelines are in place to protect both the visitors and the historical site. Pay attention to signs and follow instructions from staff members. Your cooperation is crucial for the preservation efforts.

Contribute to Preservation Efforts

Consider donating to preservation projects or volunteering if such opportunities are available. Your contributions can make a significant impact on maintaining and restoring Pompeii for future generations to explore and learn from.

CONCLUSION

As we conclude our journey through the vibrant and historic city of Pompeii, we hope that the insights and highlights provided in this guide have not only informed you but also inspired a sense of adventure and curiosity. From the majestic ruins of the ancient city that whisper stories of a civilization frozen in time, to the serene vistas of the surrounding Campanian landscape, Pompeii offers a unique window into the past coupled with the comforts and excitement of modern tourism.

This guide has taken you through the cobblestone streets of the archaeological park, where history comes alive with every step. We've explored the must-visit spots such as the Forum, the Amphitheatre, and the Villa of the Mysteries, each site offering a glimpse into the daily lives of the Pompeiians. Our culinary journey highlighted not just traditional delights but also modern eateries that offer a taste of local and international cuisines. We discussed options for family-friendly activities and romantic escapes that promise to make your stay memorable.

Whether you're a history buff, a lover of nature, or someone seeking a cultural retreat, Pompeii offers a breadth of experiences that cater to all. As you plan your visit, remember to consider the travel tips, accommodation recommendations, and best times to visit, to ensure your trip is as smooth and enjoyable as possible.

Now, with the knowledge you've gained from this guide, the stories of Pompeii are ready to be a part of your adventure. Book your trip, walk the ancient streets, and let the echoes of the past guide you through a transformative travel experience in one of Italy's most extraordinary locations. Pompeii awaits to tell you its tales in person and ensure your journey will be cherished forever. Let the adventure begin!

Made in the USA
Monee, IL
23 September 2024